Hoodwink

Tobey Truestory

First Published 2015 by Lulu
2nd Edition published 2021

www.lulu.com

ISBN: 978-1-257-16145-4

Printed in the U.S.A.

As I remember it.....

The Field Boy

Before entering this stretch of plains, the merchant had heard the rumors of wolves attacking from the mountains. So when he took in the hazy landscape to either side, guessing how many times the hills curved at their tops and then dipped down only to rise again before crashing into the rock, he didn't quite get how those that warned him could be so cautious. There was so much distance to either mountain range, and even if the mangles of hills dancing under the sun's heat could hide the wolves, there was still plenty of terrain to go before any such attack from the mountains would happen. Until that moment, any traveler could keep tabs on the oncoming attack but be well on their way through the plains.

There were disadvantages here. If one was walking, then they'd have a harder time outrunning the eventual attack, and there were no trees to climb. Yet, he figured that any traveler who decided to go this way would have a cart and horse as aid to even consider the idea.

He was one such traveler carrying lightweight goods, and even though he had one horse, he was confident in speed. He had a good strong healthy horse. And if things got rough, he had a muzzle loader just within reach underneath the tarp. There were five shells in all that he kept in his pocket. He put them there just before he started across these plains. It wouldn't take him long to load the first shot, and since he would have time to do so, he counted on that first shot to scare any wolves away.

So he road on, eyes ahead, watching the horizon roll toward him with endless expanses of grass and made occasional glances at either mountain range, mostly because he found their sight breathtaking. He saw no wolves.

When he gazed forward again, he spotted what he never expected. Even in the center of these plains the ground dipped into wide hills at times. He was at the top of one. At the top of the hill before him was a small gathering of sheep. From this distance, he counted about five of them.

Off to the right sat a boy dressed in a long brown robe with the hood pushed back to rest at his shoulders.

He could have called out to the boy, but he thought he might've spooked the sheep. Besides, he figured the boy knew he was there. So, he decided to wait until they were face-to-face to talk. Before the merchant arrived, he heard something on the wind. Something like a song. Not whistled. Not hummed either. But like a soft buzz. A mellow but cheerful tune. A little song. One that at first sounded so out of place, almost minute between the hills at the feet of the colossal rocks who were pushed from the mind by the haze. Yet, the song was above everything, a part of the wind, the currents that couldn't be caged by the majesty defining this valley.

When the merchant neared the top of that next hill, he saw that it was indeed the boy making the music. He had a small blade of grass held across his lips by his index and middle finger. As he buzzed his lips, the blade of grass sang.

The merchant brought his cart and horse to a stop.

"Good day." he said.

A breeze swept the top of the hill, ruffling the boy's bushy hair into his eyes. He smiled against the blade of grass.

"I'm surprised anyone would even want to keep a herd of sheep out here." the merchant said.

The boy lowered the blade from his mouth.

"You're pretty brave." the merchant finished.

Still gazing away from the merchant and toward the mountains, the boy smiled, "There's plenty of room out here. No one within miles. The spoils I happen upon are mine for the taking."

"I'll bet," the merchant chuckled, "but still, you aren't afraid?"

"Of what?" the boy asked.

"Why, the wolves." the merchant said.

"Wolves?" the boy asked.

"Yeah. Don't you know about the wolves?" the merchant asked.

The boy chuckled, "Yeah, I know of them. Anyone who wants to travel these plains hear about the wolves. They're warned. Just like you were. And wouldn't you know it? They still brave the stretch of green."

"So, you've seen others?" the merchant asked.

Still smiling, still gazing toward the mountains, the boy said, "Yeah, a few."

"Recently?" the merchant asked.

"No." the boy answered.

"How long have you grazed these plains?" the merchant asked.

The boy's smile widened, "Never really kept up with that. Never cared."

"Ah," the merchant said, sharing the view on the one side of the plains with the boy, "I guess, spending time out here, your mind would be on things other than time."

"You could say that." the boy said.

The merchant observed the small herd of sheep. "I don't mean to pry, but, has your herd always been this small?"

"Does one need a big herd to tend?" the boy asked.

"No," the merchant answered, "reason why I asked is that I figured you might've lost some to the wolves."

The boy didn't respond. He just kept staring at the mountains. The merchant looked and fancied their white tops, marveling at the display of extremes from cold rock to warm lush grass.

"I guess I kind of figured you'd have run into the wolves a time or two while out here, and I wouldn't be surprised if you've lost some."

"Not a one." the boy answered.

"That's outstanding." the merchant said. "So, how have you managed?"

"I know these plains." the boy answered. "I know where to be when opportunities arise."

"Like what type of opportunities?" the merchant asked.

"Where the food is." the boy said. Then he added, "...for the sheep."

The merchant nodded, "I see."

"It's a game, really." the boy continued. "Kind of like the games I assume you play at the market you're no doubt going to to sell your goods. I wonder, would you tell me what you're carrying?"

"Sure," the merchant said, aiming his thumb over his shoulder to indicate the tarp, "I'm carrying spices from my hometown. The people behind me are my regulars, you see, but when I heard about the chance before me, I couldn't hesitate."

"What chance is that?" the boy asked.

"Normally, I never bother with any town that's too far out of range, but I was told about the traveling nomads visiting these neighboring regions. They won't come any closer than the town beyond these plains, and this stretch is the quickest way to get there since their time this close is so short. These nomads like to trade, and I've been told they're partial to meat, so I made sure to bring plenty of Rosemary and Garlic. I also brought along some Juniper Berries that could be crushed for game they catch along their journey, and Paprika, because, well, it's always good to have some of that."

The boy let the blade of grass flutter from his fingers, and he got to his feet. He looked at the man, but his bushy hair was still covering his eyes. Still smiling, he said, "Well, you don't miss a thing, do you?"

"Guess I figured I'd be more successful if I was better prepared." the merchant said.

"Prepared, indeed." the boy said and approached. "People appreciate those who provide favors for them. And since you've claimed to have plenty of spice on hand," he stopped by the horse and placed his hand upon its thick shoulder, "those you happen along are very fortunate, indeed."

The merchant grinned.

"Tell ya what, though," the boy said, "I'm a bit prepared myself."

"Oh?" the merchant said.

The boy took the cloak he was wearing between his fingers and lifted it a bit, "Once you know how to sew, all you need is the wool, right?" He pointed his thumb over his shoulder at the sheep. "That part's covered, but to be totally prepared, you'd need the whole ensemble, right?"

The merchant looked down to see that the boy wasn't wearing any shoes, "What else do you mean?"

The boy lifted his hand and turned it back and forth, wiggling his fingers, "I mean this."

A howl came from the merchant's right and, for the first time since he met the boy, he glanced in the direction of those mountains. He saw the pack of wolves, having already left those rolling hills behind and was mere seconds away. He gasped and looked at the boy who was now holding a piece of the horse's harness in his mouth.

The merchant trembled in his seat.

"Those people before you I mentioned," the boy said after spitting the piece of leather from his mouth, "they provided for me as well." He reached up and grabbed at his cheek. He dug his fingers in and then pulled, tearing the flesh away without so much as a cry. The merchant cried out, though, especially when he saw the dark fur underneath and the long line of razor-sharp teeth.

Then the boy lifted his head enough to expose his eyes. Those black vertical slits widened just before he leapt at the merchant and was soon joined by the rest of the pack.

The Field Girl

The wind swirled across the hills and then dipped down into the field, ruffling the girl's robes about her face. When the wind left for the other side of the field, her robes settled, revealing her unwavering smirk as she strolled onward. She traveled alone, carrying nothing save for the clothes she wore, but it was eagerness that carried *her*.

She was in the town now at her back when residents spoke of the merchant that planned to pass through the field. "It was quicker that way", he had told them. Despite the warnings, he went. He didn't believe in the wolves.

"The wolves?" she then asked the gossipers.

Surely wolves weren't that big a deal to a merchant and a wagon, especially since they said he traveled during broad daylight. And what of this field? Isn't any field with green grass the ideal place for shepherds and their herds? Were there no shepherds in this town? There was wool and meat. Was it all imported?

And why a field? Wolves like to sneak through the forests at night, correct?

"No shepherds graze that field." a store clerk told her.

She found herself caught by the look on the clerk's face. Sensing the severity, she said, "Tell me of these wolves, then."

"Magicians. Tricksters. Demons." The clerk instantly unloaded.

The girl laughed at these descriptions.

"You would laugh," the clerk said, "but you would find that no one from the surrounding towns travel that field. The long way doesn't sound so bad if it means living longer."

"But, sir," the girl laughed, throwing back her hood, revealing her light blue hair, and her eyes sparkling as if on fire. She smiled a wicked smile, "I am a magician and a trickster. Some have even called me a demon out of fear or lack of understanding."

It was true her features were exotic enough to give him slight pause, but he didn't give the reaction most would give when astonished. Instead, he waited.

To prove herself, she grabbed the edge of her robe and whipped it about her. The robe tightened so tight that, to the clerk's understanding, there was no way she could still be bound within it. Then, the robe bundled itself up in mid-air so small that there was no way it could still be the same robe. At last, the robe relaxed, unfolding itself, but all the material that was left was enough to be a small red handkerchief.

The clerk as well as other onlookers watched in silence as the handkerchief fluttered on the wind and then settled on the ground.

"You see?" came a voice in the clerk's right ear.

He gasped and turned about to see the girl standing behind him, giving him that same wicked smile.

While the small group stood frozen silent, someone stepped forth.

"My lady," said a young boy with dark red hair, "are you able to transform yourself, say, into an animal?"

"But am I not already an animal?" she asked.

The young boy blushed. Yet, he still had courage to ask, "How are we to know this appearance is your true form?"

"Maybe this will prove it." she said and walked over to the young boy. She bent down and gave him a kiss on the cheek.

He could smell her perfume, feel her moist lips, her soft nose against his cheek.

When he looked into her eyes, he almost squinted at their brightness, but again, he kept his courage.

"What do you think now?" she asked.

Indeed, he stirred the way a young boy would from a woman's kiss. There was no mistake.

"This is the real you." he said.

"But who's to say I couldn't transform myself into, say, a wolf?"

"Could you?" the young boy asked.

"I betcha I could." she said. "In fact, I'm more than certain I'm not the only one who can." She looked at the clerk. "Which is more evidence that people do not fear wolves but men or women who can transform into wolves."

"Is it possible?" the clerk asked.

"For a free night at your Inn, I will bring back proof of my claim." she said.

"You would do that?" the young boy asked. "Battle other magicians?"

"If there is one thing a magician can't pass up, it's the thought of another who is better. There's no way I can make money here by entertaining you if you already fear other magicians who entertain themselves. Therefore, I shall confront them and show you all who the better magician is."

"You'll go alone?" the young boy asked.

"Only a magician can best another magician. If you want to fight a magician, learn a trick or two. Then I myself might take you up on a challenge."

She picked up the red handkerchief from the ground and gave it to the young boy.

Then she left the blushing boy and the clerk and those who watched her disappear and headed for the field.

For a while now, she traveled without seeing anyone. Then she saw a small herd of sheep sitting at the top of a hill.

"I see." she snickered.

When she got close enough, she saw the boy sitting in the middle of the herd. Before she reached the hill, she heard a song on the air. The small high-pitched buzz of a light and slow melody. Calm, like the wind, like the field.

She kept her stride as she studied the song. Was it a spell? Was this the trigger of some sort of illusion? If so, because she was aware of this was enough to ward off any effects.

What was the boy using to play the song? She could see that he had one hand to his mouth. A small instrument. Simple. A buzz.

"Ha!" she laughed to herself. "A blade of grass."

Even a magician could weave a spell from a blade of grass, but there was nothing in those notes that tickled her senses. It was just a nice song for a nice day. Something to pass the time.

Yet, as she got closer, her senses tickled. The boy, no, it wasn't a boy, a creature, a wolf? It was smiling at her. Of course, it knew she was coming for a while now, but how far out was she before it noticed? That was key in this setup.

Nevertheless, she strolled up the hill to meet this challenge.

Before any words were exchanged, she observed the sheep, mindless in their grazing. Mindless was right. They weren't sheep. No grass was being consumed. Though, one would have to pay attention to such little details to notice this. These sheep, they were illusions.

She stopped at the edge of the herd. From there, she could see the boy's grin. He had long since stopped playing his calm melody.

"So," she said, "are you really a wolf or is that what you use to scare people?"

The boy's grin didn't falter. He turned his face in her direction and lifted his head to where she could see his eyes underneath his bushy bangs. Sure enough, they were the yellow eyes and black vertical slits of a wolf's.

The boy sniffed the air twice and then said, "You smell funny."

"Heh, whatever you are, you do have a keen sense of smell." the girl said. "Way to live up to your reputation, but what I want to know is who taught you how to create an almost flawless illusion?"

The boy's eyes flickered at the sheep and then settled back on the girl. "Will this be a competition of wits or physical strength?"

"Either way is fine with me." the girl said.

"I can only assume since you've come to call me out." the boy said. "But I'm curious as to why. Surely, you're not one who's blinded with delusions of justice."

"No doubt you have murdered people, and I'm guessing you did so in order to eat, but in order for *me* to enjoy a meal, I have to remove the competition."

"Ah, flattery." the boy said. "It begins with wits. Plan to throw me off guard first, but, poor girl, you are unarmed. All you have is a trick."

"I won't deny what I am." she said.

"Was that a verbal blow?" the boy chuckled. "But I will say that you and I could be on equal ground."

"And how is that?" she asked.

"You saw through my illusion," the boy said getting to his feet, letting the blade of grass flutter from his fingers, "and I...have seen through yours."

The girl hunched down, readying herself, grabbing at the edges of her cloak.

"That won't help you." the boy snickered, and turned completely around, facing another girl in the same robes with the same shining eyes.

Both identical girls gasped when the snout of the wolf ripped from the boy's face. The true girl before him jumped several steps back and flung her robes forward.

The robes weaved themselves around the wolf's throat just as he sunk his teeth into the girl's right arm. She screamed. He laughed, but his laughter was cut short. The robes tightened.

Now both stood upon that hill locked onto one another, both grinning.

"That...nose of yours." the girl grunted.

"You were..." the boy coughed through his clenched teeth, "armed...after all."

"You...gah!...shouldn't be...so surprised." the girl winced. "False clothing and all."

"Nor you." the boy grunted, "Little...details, right?"

"Illusions...and fake clothing." the girl snickered, "We *are* on...equal ground."

"In...hck!...more ways...than...one." the boy said, his yellow eyes rolling back in his head.

"How's...that?" the girl asked.

"Neither...one...loses." the boy sighed and then slumped in the grip of her robes. When his teeth were free, the girl threw him off and examined her arm. The wolf boy lay dead at her feet, but the wound on her arm was turning a dark purple.

She gasped, grasping her bleeding arm, and dropped to her knees. Not only was there pain in her arm but also in her mouth. She reached up and touched her teeth, gasping when she felt two razor sharp canines protruding from her other teeth.

She chuckled at the little wolf boy and said, "Touché."

The Young Hero

Now he walked the field. He came here despite what they said, and he left that town without them knowing. He carried with him only one thing and that was the handkerchief she gave to him before she left.

The handkerchief was half the reason why he set out across the field. The other reason, well...

Before he left, he waited like everyone else for her to return with the proof she said she'd bring: proof that they were being deceived by mere men and women. He didn't expect her to return that night. The field was long and wide. Yet, the next day, fewer and fewer people expected her to appear. The numbers dwindled to just he and the store clerk.

He sat at the quaint wooden bar along the outer edge of the store with a mug full of water sitting neglected beside his elbow.

The clerk noticed the young boy's head hanging down, his focus on something else. When the clerk stepped closer, he saw that the young boy was hovering over the handkerchief.

The clerk sighed and said, "Ain't no sense in killing yourself over it. It was just a kiss on the cheek and a spooky handkerchief."

"Heh," the boy said, "spooky, huh?"

"Pardon?" the clerk asked.

"Watch." the boy said.

He was twirling his finger around inside the handkerchief. When about half the handkerchief was tight about his finger, he picked his hand up. The handkerchief followed, the other end lying limp in the air.

Then, the boy smirked and flicked his wrist, turning his palm upward, curling his fingers inward but keeping his index finger extended. The limp cloth flicked upward as well, hardening into a long shape that was more like an extension of the boy's finger. Yet, at the end, it made a point that one would gather was sharp, despite being nothing more than cloth.

"Spooky handkerchief indeed." the boy said, turning the claw-like extension downward. He touched it to the surface of the wooden bar. Then he raked it slowly across. The cloth carved a fine and shallow groove out of the wood.

The clerk gasped and stumbled backward, nearly tripping over a box of tomatoes.

When he gathered himself, he leaned close to the boy and whispered, "I thought it was just the girl who was magic."

"I've been messing around with this handkerchief ever since she left," the boy explained, "keeping in mind her offer of challenging me some day if I learned a trick or two. I found out the handkerchief itself was magic, so I've been able to learn a trick or two."

"You're not thinking about going, are you?" the clerk whispered.

"I wonder why it was she gave *me* the handkerchief instead of someone else. I thought maybe it was because I was the one who showed the most interest in her world. Seems curiosity alone can be a key to get you into all sorts of things."

"But, if she went to challenge them, why do you think you aught to go seek to challenge her?" the clerk asked.

"Maybe I won't have to challenge her," the boy said, "but I at least want to find out what happened to her."

"But why?" the clerk asked.

"Well, since the handkerchief is magic," the boy chuckled, "don't you suppose her kiss was as well?"

"Now that's just plain ole women's charm." the clerk said. "Tis a spell as old as time. Nothing new like that handkerchief."

The boy stood from his chair, "Then how could I resist a spell so engraved in our world that we've yet to find a way to counter it?"

"It's a fool's errand." the clerk warned him.

"Isn't that what we call love?" the boy said.

"But what about the wolves?" the clerk asked.

"If they are really men and women, then I fear them not." the boy said.

Not long after that, he slipped away from the town, and now here he was, walking the silent field. He kept the handkerchief bound around his right hand, like a fingerless glove, but he wasn't using the cloth's magic to do so. The knot that kept the cloth firmly bound rested in his palm.

He remembered the first tingly feeling he got from her visit was from her kiss. The second was from the handkerchief when he finally got it to do what he wanted it to do. He felt a similar tingly feeling now, but unlike the first two, he didn't enjoy this one.

"You. Boy." came a dark voice from his side.

He stopped and noticed for the first time that he was surrounded by five figures dressed in brown cloaks. Their faces were hidden under their hoods.

"Are you the one who slew our friend?" another of them asked.

"You, who walks this field without fear." another said.

"With eyes forward and chin up." another added.

The boy studied these figures a moment, noticing how they all were standing upright and on two feet like men, noting how they were a little taller than he was, a height that matched their dark voices.

"Was your friend male or female?" he decided to ask.

The figures chuckled.

"The young warrior has seen much battle to forget which prey fell at what time." one snickered.

"Okay," the boy said, "let me ask you this then: Was your friend man or wolf?"

More chuckles from the figures.

"He was of *us*." one answered.

"And you are men." the boy said.

"Are we men...?" another chuckled.

"Or are we wolves?" another asked.

"You look and sound like men to me." the boy said.

"But what does this boy fear more?" one asked.

"You would take on the image of what I fear?" The boy asked. "Is that how you do it?"

"We *do* nothing." one said. "We just *are*."

"Just men." the boy scoffed.

"Don't be so quick to judge." one said.

They all reached up and pulled back their hoods. Indeed, they had the heads and faces of men, but their eyes were yellow, their pupils vertical black slits, and when they smiled, they exposed two razor sharp teeth longer than the rest.

"Now, what say you, boy?" one asked.

"Hmph. Men and their parlor tricks." the boy said.

"You saying you won't even believe your own eyes?" another asked.

"What would this be?" another questioned, "A hallucination or five beasts in human clothing?"

"I would go with hallucination." the boy said. "Something I can't smell in the air that makes me see what you want me to see."

"So sure, he is." one of them chuckled.

"It's how he feels every time he confronts his opponents." another said.

"You want to know how your friend was killed?" the boy decided to play his cards now. He raised his hand that was bound in the hand-kerchief. "It was by this."

He didn't even have to speak. The handker-chief obeyed his unspoken command and un-tied itself from his palm. It twisted about his index finger, shaping itself into the claw like it did before. The boy kept his hand there for them all to see.

"Unlike your tricks, this is real magic."

All their eyes were locked upon the sharp-ened handkerchief.

Good, the boy thought, you play your game of fear, then so will I. But unlike you, I have the advantage.

"Stupid boy." one of them hissed.

The boy glanced to his left. The man there was raising a hand to his face. "The bad part about all this," the man said, "is that you've been wrong all this time." The man hooked a finger inside his mouth and then pulled. His cheek tore easy enough, but that wasn't what gripped the boy's attention. It was the fur that shown underneath the cheek.

The man kept pulling, tearing his cheek away to reveal the rest of his hairy face and then one single wolf ear that jumped up as soon as it was freed from its fleshly prison. The human ear on the side of the man's face was torn in half as nothing but a decoration.

"This is what really lies beneath our deceit." the wolf man snickered.

Stay calm, the boy told himself. Stay calm. They are like her, magicians with tricks. Nothing more. "I don't doubt your heart is full of craftiness and malice. Nice analogy. *I* stand before you as who I am," then he wiggled the handkerchief claw, "with something more."

"How fitting that it would be a claw." the wolf man said, "This beast against these. We *will* avenge our fallen comrade."

The wolf man dashed at the young boy.

What else was the boy to do except fight back? He wasn't afraid, but he knew he wasn't someone who was capable of fighting these men. He didn't know why he knew this, but he knew it wasn't because of being outnumbered.

Whatever they were, men devoted to some cause, he was just a boy with a trick...and he would use it to his advantage.

He swung his handkerchief claw at the wolf man. He was thought to be a warrior, so the wolf man acted accordingly and took the attack serious. He ducked underneath the handkerchief claw, but he didn't duck low enough.

Despite what the boy saw at that moment, the wolf man was more worried about landing his own blow, and so he struck the boy in the side as he passed.

The boy doubled up and stumbled forward.

The wolf man landed behind him and turned about for a second strike, but something made him pause.

The boy was laughing on his way to the ground. He caught himself from falling face first.

The five men listened to the boy chuckle to himself.

"I knew it." the boy finally said.

He chuckled some more.

"Get up, boy." the wolf man snapped.

The boy looked up at the wolf man, still chuckling. "You're just men with tricks."

The wolf man grinned, "Still audacious, I see. A stubborn warrior. This fight will stretch out to entertain us all."

"No," the boy chuckled. "The fight is over."

"Still have trouble believing your own eyes? You're the one on the ground, boy." the wolf man chuckled.

"But I've won." the boy said.

"And how is that?" the wolf man asked.

"I proved you wrong." the boy said. "You may have gotten your blow in, but I got mine in as well."

"What are you talking about?" the wolf man asked.

"Yeah, boy," another said, "he ducked underneath your blow."

"The boy's blind with pride." another chuckled.

"No." the boy said, "I hit your ear, wolf man. Didn't you feel it?"

The wolf man frowned.

"Of course you didn't." the boy said. He pushed himself to his feet. "And that's because your ear is fake. My claw went straight through your ear, but instead of piercing it, or you yourself bending your ear to protect it since it should have been a natural part of your body you'd want to protect, but my claw passed right through just as if I had cut through thin air."

All the men gasped.

The boy felt two hands settle on his shoulders. He froze.

"Thank you." came a familiar voice in his ear.

Without turning his head, the boy whispered back, "It's you."

She giggled, "Is it?"

Someone latched onto the man in the back of the group. This other person leapt onto the man's shoulders, taking his head in their hands, and leaning down to bite him in the neck.

He cried and shuffled about, trying to pull the person off him, but the extra weight toppled them both to the ground. The other figure landed on their feet while the bitten man crashed on his side. He put a hand to his neck, groaning.

The crouching figure wasted no time, springing onto the nearest man, covering his head with their body and biting him on the neck.

One of the other men rushed at his comrade's aid. The person above flung out their arm, sending a length of their robes toward that approaching man. The robes wrapped around his neck and started squeezing.

Now another rushed at the figure.

The figure pulled their mouth from their prey in a spray of blood and jumped onto the other who was being strangled by the robes. Their feet crashed into the strangling man's chest, pushing him down on the ground.

The robes released him, and the figure cart wheeled from the man's chest, catching the approaching men in the chin with her feet.

All that was left standing was the wolf man himself.

"You!" he cried. "You've become! Why do you...?"

The figure just stood there, grinning at the wolf man who suddenly felt a sharp jab in his back. The jab went deep into his body, and he coughed.

When he looked over his shoulder, he saw the boy. The boy was gripping his right forearm with his left hand. His right hand was hidden within the man's cloak.

"It's...just..." the wolf man grunted, "a... ...trick..."

"What's the matter?" the other figure asked, "Don't believe your own eyes?"

The boy pulled his hand free and stepped back. The wolf man saw the bloody handkerchief claw. He smiled, chuckled, and then dropped to the ground, dead.

The boy dropped to his knees. He was still gripping his forearm with his free hand. He was staring at the bloody handkerchief claw.

He just killed a man with it.

The figure walked over and knelt down in front of him. She placed a hand on his shoulder. This time, he felt the true weight of her hand.

He glanced over his shoulder, saw an empty field, and then looked into her glowing eyes.

"I haven't learned that trick yet." he snickered.

"You can." she said, and lifted his hand to put the bloody handkerchief claw between them, "Since you seem to be willing." He stared at the handkerchief again, read it again, and accepted it. He looked past it now to her. "What happened to you? You're just now finding these guys?"

"Actually, I needed your help." she said.

"*My* help?" he asked.

"Yeah. Kind of embarrassing, really, but despite all that bragging I did, one of them got the best of me."

"One of them." he said, "You mean...the one they were talking about?"

"Yeah," she said.

"What do you mean though, by 'got the best of you'?"

"We ended up fighting each other. I killed him, but he bit me before he died. He told me that we both won, and since then..." she pulled her hood back to show her face. She looked just as he remembered her. Beautiful. Then she smiled.

He saw the two fangs extending past her other teeth.

"It was all I could do to keep my sanity." she said. "It's why I didn't go back to your town."

The boy was shaking his head, refusing to believe it. "It's a trick."

"It's not a trick." she said.

"But...but...these men..."

"Had tricks," she said, "but who taught them their tricks?"

"But," the boy said, looking at her fangs, "if those aren't tricks..."

"Then there are wolves." she said.

"With magic?" he asked.

"Powerful magic." she said. "I'm becoming one of them. I can sneak into their lair, but not with my sanity." She put a hand on his shoulder. "You brought me around. You are my grip on reality."

"What are you saying?" he questioned.

"I'm saying, I need you to come with me."

"To their lair?"

"Yes," she said, "before I give in one more time."

"But," he said, "I am no fighter."

She shook her head and grabbed his wrist, bringing the bloodied claw to his attention. "Like I said before, you've got potential."

The Lair

Tracking the wolves wasn't a problem. The beasts weren't afraid of anyone, so they never tried to hide their tracks that traversed the field from the colder mountain range in the north. Though, the guts to actually hunt them, let alone confront them was in meager supply.

Yet, here traveled a boy with a woman, both wearing the hooded cloaks of those they slew, both bringing themselves to the beasts with something other than guts to boast their advance.

The sun sat upon the westernmost snow-capped peaks, stretching those jagged shadows toward the middle of the field. However, the woman waited to pull the hood from her head, feeding an instinct that harbored an affection for the dark. At the same time, she suffered from the shame the physical manifestations of this instinct expressed.

When they did slip underneath that blanket of blue green and gray, the boy glanced her way several times, wondering when she would remove her hood.

After a while without conversation, he spoke to her, "You won't look at me?"

Her hood shifted his way, but it was only a gesture of addressing him. He didn't see her eyes or her face.

"Not sure what I would see." she answered, her hood pointing forward again. "Things look strange to me now."

"Even me?" he asked.

"All things." she said. "Though, I admit, you I have not looked upon since I've noticed the changes. So, you're still a mystery."

"One you wouldn't discover?" he asked.

She laughed at that. "The world has always looked like an adventure to me, nothing barred. Everything opened." She paused before adding, "Only now do I look upon these promises without any fear at all."

"You feared before?" he asked.

"Not feared, but appreciated the challenge." she answered.

"So, there is no more challenge?" he asked.

"Let's just say the bars have been lowered." she answered. "Now I know why they don't fear. If anything could prove a challenge, it would have to be overwhelming for anyone else."

When he gave no response, she added, "But this perspective doesn't just try to antagonize the world. Like I said, I saw promises before, but where I saw some, I see many now."

He thought about his next statement, feeling the bravery in just thinking it, accented by the fluttering in his stomach, and figured that since he was already out here, going to meet a deadly adversary head on, then maybe it was in his nature to say such a statement, "Then, the curiosity of what you'll discover when you look my way is eating away at me."

She stopped in her tracks, paused, and then threw her head back with laughter.

He spread his hands to the sides, "What?"

When her jolly fit subsided, she sighed and gripped the edges of her hood. Then she pulled it from her head to reveal her blue hair. She didn't look back at him yet. He admitted to himself the anticipation he spoke of before played also on getting to see what she would look like now.

When she did turn, he readied a gasp, but the air never jumped past his lips. What he saw was the same beautiful face he met back in his home village.

Her eyes still glowed that mystic color, though behind that haze were the yellowish irises of the beasts. Still, he felt no fear. Because of the shade, her pupils weren't drawn into tight vertical slits, but were wide, resembling his, taking in the fading light. So he didn't see much change.

Then, when she grinned at him, his eyes focused on her sharpened canines, and there was something else in how her lips had curled. The gesture could have looked like a snarl.

Yet, he offered her his own smile in return, "So, what do you see?"

"Temptation." she said.

That wasn't quite what he expected. His smile dropped slightly, "Temptation?"

She turned herself toward him. "That's right." She looked him up and down, "You look...tempting." She pranced toward him, her eyes locked on his, both unblinking.

What she had in mind, he didn't know. He just stood his ground and hoped for pleasant things.

"The thing about perspective," she said, "is that whatever you see influences the way you might feel, and how you feel determines a lot in how you carry yourself."

That smile on her face sent chills down his spine. He didn't know whether that was a good thing or not.

They were true, her words. He didn't know what she would do but he couldn't help but feel like the prey no matter in what pretense. She definitely carried herself as the dominant force here.

Still, he made himself stand his ground. Even when she got right up in his face. They stared at one another for a few moments, saying nothing. Then she said, "You're trembling."

He broke from her eyes to look down at himself, "Am I?"

That's when she jumped at him. He had no time to react. He felt her and nothing but her. Her will. She decided his fate. It was all in her hands. He was so close to her, he had no room to run. All the space they both occupied was hers.

His heart raced. He was in her clutches. Her face had brushed to his left. Did she go for his neck? He was cold. Paralyzed?

Yet, in all the confusion, he knew one thing. They were both still standing. His fluttering heart settled into a fast but comfortable rhythm as the moment dragged on without a dramatic end.

She hadn't moved, instead, just held him there in her embrace. He felt heat rushing throughout his body.

She giggled. He felt her breath brushing, not against his neck, but his ear.

"Did I scare you?" she whispered.

"I...I don't know." he answered.

"Sorry." she said anyway. "I was just excited. I couldn't help myself."

Excited? His own excitement added fuel to his beating heart.

"But, you don't fear me." she said.

"I didn't think I had to." he said.

She pulled back to look into his eyes again. He wasn't trembling anymore. "That's good," she said. "because, for what we're about to do, we need to trust each other."

"Do?" he asked, a grin touching the corners of his lips.

"Why, yes." she said, patting his cheek, "We're invading their lair. Remember?"

He blinked, coming to his senses, "Oh! Oh, yeah. Yeah. That's right." He shook away his other thoughts, "I apologize."

"Don't apologize." she said. "We haven't lost to them yet."

He beamed. "You're right."

From the distance, the mountains looked almost impossible, because giants were impossible for mere humans to conquer, seeming nothing more than straight shots upward, all rock, slopes too steep, but once they got close, all those details at the base started to fill in the ranks of logic, discovering slopes that leaned further over than they had expected, forming the foothills that seemed be forever out of reach. That was, until they realized they were on top of them all this time.

The ground underneath their feet made that gradual change from the calm valley to the rocks in front of them.

As they walked, they felt like they were shrinking while the world was growing. Yes, as one would figure, the giants were impossible to conquer, for they were the whole world in which the boy and the woman walked.

The mountains knew this and showed a fraction of pity for them, though only to boast walls of rock that carved paths deep into themselves, supposedly small details but proved to dictate the fate of the travelers.

The paths liked to play with them, too, offering small patches of downward slopes among the forever struggle to get to the top. However, the boy and woman were of the opinion that they wouldn't have to go that far. The wolves no doubt thrived off pride and looked down their snouts at their prey, yet, dark deeds were dark deeds, and dark deeds required dark hearts, and dark hearts dwelled in dark places.

They looked for a cave carved into the rock, something that didn't mind being discovered but didn't go out of its way to show itself. Convenient but flowing upon a neutral standing with its abrasive surroundings. They found one during a downward slope, just before another torturing hill started its rise. That transition made up either wall of the cave's opening.

Sneaking up on the wolves had been the general idea, but both the boy and the woman knew the wolves were aware of their presence long before they found the cave.

But that was just as well. The woman could smell them, too.

"So," the boy said, "how do we do this, then?"

"We walk straight in." she said.

"To our deaths?" he questioned.

"To deliver death." she said.

"Maybe you can," he said, "but how can I?"

"A wolf's sense of smell is your toughest obstacle, yes," she said, "but also your best armor."

"How so?" he asked.

"By fooling their noses." she said.

"And how do I do that?" he asked.

"To begin," she said, "hug me."

The boy gaped at her. "Hug you?"

"Well, if you're opposed to that," she giggled, "then I shall hug you."

She slipped her arms to either side of his neck, pressed herself against him, and folded her arms about his head. For the first few seconds, the boy was stunned by the gesture, but then he relished this chance and took her in his arms. If this was really part of some plan, he held her for different reasons, and while they embraced, their dire situation waited.

"Now," she whispered into his hair, "my scent has mixed with yours."

"I see." he said after a moment, "but won't they see me anyway? Aren't we going to confront them head on?"

"We will," she said, "but we will have allies."

He looked up at her, "We will?"

"Yes," she looked down at him, "and they'll look exactly like you."

"Like me?" he asked.

She looked down at her handkerchief still bound around his right hand. "Since you learned how to use it, do you really understand how it works?"

He looked down to examine the handkerchief, "It just shapes itself into what I want."

"And the only thing you want is a claw?" she giggled.

"Well," he smirked, lowering his head, half ashamed, half proud as he looked at the handkerchief again, "it's all I've been thinking about."

"It reacts off what you know." she said. "I know myself so I can copy myself and trick their eyes and noses. Now, I know you, so I can make copies of you."

"Know me?" he asked.

"Well, your face and the parts of you I felt whenever we embraced."

She smiled at him and he blushed.

"To be able to do what I do, you have to know yourself. It happens because you're confident. You don't think about it. Thinking is prone to let doubt slip in. When you act, you do what you are capable of doing, and the cloth responds."

He was nodding at her explanation while looking at the handkerchief. Now he looked up and said, smiling, "That's kind of vague, but I guess it makes sense."

"It takes time." she said. "Nothing wrong with practice."

"I still don't grasp the mechanics of it." he said.

"You will when you realize there are no mechanics to it." she said, and as if to contradict her words, the corners of her smirk stretched a bit. He only realized this contradiction when he noticed the focus of her eyes shifted. He spun about, suddenly fearful that the enemy was behind him.

And they were.

Four of them, dressed just as he and she were, but hiding their faces. He stepped back from them and ran into her opened palm.

"What, afraid of your own shadow?" she asked.

"What?" he gasped, not taking his eyes off them.

"Go take a look." she said.

He glanced over his shoulder at her, questioning.

"Go lift up their hoods, see yourself looking back." She gave him a little shove. He wasn't ready for it and stumbled before he balanced himself. Then, he just stood there before the four enemies. They stood there staring back, although this was just a guess. They had to be staring at him, because their hoods were pointed his way. They didn't attack. Didn't move. Just stood. Waiting.

The boy didn't approach them.

"I asked you once if you were afraid." she said. "You told me you didn't think you had to be."

He understood what she meant, gathered his courage, and approached one of the enemies in the middle, though his hesitation now was rooted in the idea of pulling up the hood and seeing his own face. Looking in a mirror was one thing, because the reflection was your own and you controlled it. How would he react to someone else wearing his exact face?

He stood before the one on the left. The hood was lowered enough to where all he could see was the person's chin. Was it his chin? He couldn't tell, but what unnerved him was that this person didn't react to his presence. Neither did the other three. They stood like statues, having no life, yet borrowing an existence...but what would they do with it?

They remained clueless as the boy reached toward the one before him and took the edge of the hood in his fingers. He felt then that these *were* statues, not alive, not copies of himself. So, he lifted the hood without hesitation, and then his fingers shook. They shook so bad that the hood slipped from his grasp, and he stepped back, shuddering.

"Or, maybe you are afraid." the girl said.

The once hooded person reflected each and every feature that made up the boy's face. So much so that the boy found himself motivated to question memories of his own reflection. The pride of his existence stomped its way forward. It may have looked just like him, but there was no life in its features. No expression. No thoughts. Just existing.

"Who knows?" the girl said, and he felt her hands on his shoulders, "Maybe you'll know who you really are after all this."

The boy swallowed to feel his own life, and nodded, "Maybe so."

◎

Six shadows walked down into hell. They were shadows only, because there was no light, nothing to give them form. They were just hints, but they made sounds as they descended the corridor of rock. She led him, because she could see, and the other false existences followed without question, without sight. Without life.

They held each other's hand and walked side-by-side, she and the boy. There were no words. Just the sound of their feet crunching the grains underneath.

How? the boy wondered. How will this play out? If the wolves attacked now, he would be useless. Yet, just as he entertained the thought, a prick of light touched his vision. It was a soft glow. Red and fuzzy. Right there in front of his face, or so he thought. There was no depth perception. Not until his feet took him a bit further, and the light revealed more.

He saw the shadows of crevasses tucked in among the texture of the corridor walls. Those walls reached toward him, building the corridor in his sight. He glanced to his left and saw her, well, the front edge of her hood and her robes. He looked down at his right hand to see the handkerchief wrapped around his palm. He flexed his fingers once, readying himself. Then he felt her squeeze his other hand and looked her way again.

Her hood was turned his way. He could see the edge of the side facing the light, but her face wasn't there. It was hidden in the black hole that peered back at him. Yet, he saw the faint bluish glow of her eyes, nothing more than ghosts somewhere far away, and he tried to swallow.

"Not yet." she whispered from that space.

He wondered if she saw the same thing when she looked at him but without the ghosts of his eyes. He nodded anyway, and apparently she saw his gesture, because she gazed forward again. He looked into the small light ahead.

It was different now.

It was looking back at them, an eye of red with a pitch-black pupil in the center, a vertical slit like that of the wolves.

The boy held in a gasp and started to stop, when the girl's grip on his hand didn't loosen as she kept her pace, tugging him with her.

"Not yet." she whispered again.

He didn't feel himself regain his pace. He just saw the eye ahead. The pupil standing there, a figure with broad shoulders and muscular arms, wild hair that stood up straight, and claws at the ends of its fingers.

It took two steps forward.

"Not yet." she whispered again.

The figure crouched down. Then it melted. Melted? No. It shifted. Shifted where? How? When? There! The other side! Against the wall. Moving again! Here! Now!

The red light was taken by a wall of black. The figure jumped at him. He saw nothing. Felt nothing, just heard the muscle behind its weight, the speed, the opening of its jaws, the claws cutting the air.

Then he felt her, her robes, her wind brushing him from the left. Then he heard grains crunching at his feet. He heard an opened mouth snarl, a snarl that never shut but stopped nonetheless. He heard her grunt. He heard something beating against something else. Then he heard something sag.

She sighed.

She knelt down and the red light at the end of the corridor rolled back into view. He looked down to see her silhouette shift before him. He stood frozen in place, though. He wanted to know what she did, what happened, but he couldn't move. The corridor kept silent around them. He forgot about the four false existences behind him.

She stood and blocked the red light. When she spoke, he could tell she was facing him. "Let's go." She turned to the left and took a few steps that way before continuing toward the red light. "Oh," she looked back and whispered, "and watch your step."

He looked down and saw a black spot along the corridor floor in front of him. That was all he could make out. His heart was pumping in his chest, but he stepped around the spot and followed after her.

Moments down the corridor without a word, the four false existences passed him up and walked ahead of the girl. He didn't ask what was going on since she never deviated from her pace. But the red light ahead was growing and filling out to be a passage that curved to the left.

There was only one choice, one direction, one way. No deviations. They were going to face their adversaries head on. Of course, he knew this from the start, but approaching the moment made it real. Made it final, when all it had been was something he had yet to reach but was sure to reach it at some point. Now that they were here, he felt all sorts of wrong, like they were in the wrong place, like their true goal might've been somewhere else, or that they were approaching it wrong.

And just as if to test his doubts, she stopped.

So did the false existences.

She looked back at him, and he saw only the ghosts of her eyes in that dark place.

"This is it." she said.

He said nothing. Just stared into her ghostly eyes.

"Think about nothing. Pay attention to every-thing. Listen for everything. Don't stop moving. Don't stop fighting. No matter what happens.

You and I came here to beat them. It doesn't matter what or who they are. We came here to win. We walk out alive. You walk out when everything is over. I'll walk out when it's over. Don't doubt. Don't ask questions. Just act. Don't stop acting until it's just you and me left. Understand?"

He understood. His beating heart told him he understood how real this was. How fast it all might happen. How fast he wanted it to happen. How he wanted it to be over with already. How much he was about to be absent from himself. How he was about to become something he only tasted back in the field when those five confronted him. He was not afraid of those, but what lie in wait here, these were the true creatures. The source of the fear that sealed the field off from travelers.

He and the girl ventured into it. They might as well become it, right?

"Just remember one thing." she said. "We'll be together no matter what."

He smiled at that and nodded, too afraid to speak in those hidden shadows. He loosened his fingers and let the handkerchief shape itself into the claw. He bounced on the balls of his feet, readying himself.

"We go!" she hissed into that corridor, and she was a breeze, flap of clothing, a jerk into the light, and he was an idea in motion.

He rounded the corner, and she might have been gone, she might have been at his side, but nothing had a shape. There was light all around him. Red light. Perfect color. Then there were the dark shapes. There were differences from the creatures and her. She was gray. They were black. As long as he didn't attack the gray he would be alright. As for the false existences, they were nothing but blurs zipping about having no solid presence, just sweeping motions. Sometimes those dark shapes would fall to those sweeping motions. Sometimes they wouldn't. Sometimes he would see himself moving toward one of those dark spots, though he couldn't feel himself attacking. He just knew he was. He was using his claw.

There was shouting. Howling. Growling, cutting noises, ripping noises, stomping noises, grunts, and he didn't know if any of it was him. He forgot a lot of things in that short period of time, but as reality happened around them, incasing this moment in its own separate existence within the world, time streamed by his eyes in fragments of visuals:

Yellow eyes wide and full of rage.
Teeth glinting red. Covered in blood?
Claws extended, swiping at the air.
Laughter.
Blood flying like a crimson ribbon.

Fur. Far away and up close.
Collisions that turned the red off at times.
Turning.
His claw.
Swiping!
Turning. Turning!
His claw again.
Stabbing!
Clothes flapping.
A great wind.
Shouting.
Tearing.
Ghosts floating and zipping about, not making
sense.
Sweat.
Stumbling. Something on the ground.
Bodies.
Opened snouts, tongues hanging out to the side.
Frozen expressions. Human or wolf? Or both?
Rage! More rage! Movement! Spitting. Panting.
Breathing. Red everywhere. Stone underneath.
Knees against stone. Painful to stand. Blurry.
Hunching over. Weight on his back. Pain some-
where. Biting. Claw reaching. Awkward angle.
Connection. A yelp. No more weight.
Standing. Moving! There! Here! At the side!
Where is she? No thinking! Blood! Pain! Red
doused in black paint smeared and erased.
Smudged.

Crouching. Pouncing. Ghosts! Tasting. Claws glinting red white. Collision. Face against rock. No panic. Just movement. Keep moving. Pain. Ignored. Claw moving, catching! A yelp! A splash of blood. More tasting. More smelling. Where was he? Where was this? How deep? How far? Where's the end?
No! No thinking!
Swing! Swing! Decorate the red! Let it all be red! Not black smudges. No black shapes. Let the ghosts stay. Let the gray stay. Let her laughter stay. Let the accusing go. Let the rage go. Let the disgust go. Let the outrage go.
Turn! Turn! Swing! Swing! And then see the writhing thing!

A moment captured within a moment. A part that was still. He didn't think it was possible. But he couldn't focus on it, and something made him want to focus. Yet, the only way to do that would be to become still as well, but she said don't stop moving.

He didn't stop. Couldn't stop. The motions changed, though. The red shot past him, bringing the writhing thing toward him. Was it he who was moving or it? There was no way of knowing. A part of him was just satisfied by this approach. He'd soon know what the writhing thing was.

It was black like the others. So it was bad. But it didn't move like the others. The writhing was its own battle. A lone battle. A battle against itself, and the boy found out why.

When the red stopped flowing, and the writhing thing stopped where it was that certain distance away, he saw it lying on the rocky floor. Its arms and legs were contorted. So was its face. Or was that its face? Something was trying to take this thing over. The boy could see it spreading over the thing's body. But it wasn't a material. It was understood. A change in the gestures that opposed that of the thing's need to writhe. Where this other covered the thing's body there was calm. Acceptance.

But that was wrong. This control, this covering agent. It was wrong. The writhing thing was correct to writhe. The calmness was a sort of death. An inescapable death. That wasn't the right death. Death was a release. Not a cage.

And so, the boy thought one single thought there in that moment within a moment. He brought motion into the stillness and plunged his claw into the writhing thing's chest.

The covering agent shot out of the thing's body like a fleeing virus. The boy could feel that, because he felt the need to writhe coming back to the thing. But it didn't last for long. The writhing stopped. The thing's body was fixed into a contortion. Frozen. Then it relaxed.

This was a different relaxation. This was a release. The boy gave the thing the correct death.

That's when the chanting stopped.

That's when the motion stopped. That's when the red came into focus. The boy looked at the cave walls, studying their heights, the ceiling above, the stalactites hanging down. Then he felt the heat.

He turned to that heat and saw the large flame in the center of the lair. It was seated in the middle of a shallow pit bordered by stones. The smoke gathered around the stalactites, but the boy could smell the aroma. The smell of burning flesh.

He felt his stomach heave. He was already on his knees. He didn't remember being on his knees, but it was fortunate because he lurched forward, catching himself with his hands and vomited.

All of it that happened, all of it that he could remember came back to him now. It was all pushed along by the rush of heat and adrenaline. Now he was coming down off the rush. His body shuddered. Weakened. He glanced at his right hand to see the claw still attached to his finger. The handkerchief was already red, but now it was soaked in a darker red. So was his hand. His forearm.

What else of his was red?

A dark spot within the red loomed over him, arms raised, eyes glinting, a knife grasped in both hands. He didn't see it. Didn't hear it. Not until the thing took in a hissing breath to deliver the blow.

He jerked his head toward the sound. Saw the figure over him. Saw the knife. He tugged at his body, but there was no strength.

The knife came down.

The gray appeared, streaking into the black, taking the black away to uncover the red once again.

The boy flinched at the quick change in color. Then he heard the collision on the rocky floor near him. He looked and saw the gray and black, a bundle that didn't move. Though, it shuddered. Then he saw a hand fall, heard the knife hit the rocky floor, the sound of giving in.

Then the gray rose from the black. Her hood had been taken down from her head during the foray. A slip of blue sat upon the gray. Then she turned her head, and he saw her face and her ghostly eyes.

They experienced the moment for a time, staring at each other, realizing the other, accepting the outcome, glad of the outcome.

"How did you do it?" she asked in that red stillness.

He blinked, his breathing settling, "What?"

"How did you cure him?" she asked and pointed at the thing that once writhed but rested now. He looked at the thing, considered what she was asking, and then looked at her. But before he could answer, she was crawling toward him on her hands and knees.

"Me next." she said.

"What are you...?" he gasped when she pounced upon him and shoved him on his back against the rocky floor. She hovered over him.

"Cure me." she said.

His mouth moved to respond, but he said nothing. Cure? Had something been cured already?

"What was it?" she asked. "How did you do it?"

Again, he faltered, still reeling from the afterglow.

"Please." she said. "Won't you cure me?"

The Cure

"Did you see it happening?" she asked, but he didn't hear the question.

He felt her voice. It brushed at his face along with her drooping hair. It saved him from what he saw, but he didn't know she saw the same thing.

The blood of victims.

The sequences were catching up to him. Somehow he had beat them here and forgot about them, but the blood splattered on her face brought him pause long enough to be caught. Only then had he realized what he did. What they *both* did.

And she had asked...

He started to nod, but she glanced over her shoulder and nodded toward something.

His eyes trailed that way, and he saw the other half of the bundle, the black half. It was pulsing with a fading life, a harsh breathing.

What had it been before? He shuffled through the bombarding memories and remembered a dark figure looming over him, wielding a knife. Then she tackled it, saving him.

There it lay, dying.

"You heard him, right?" she asked, still watching it breathe. "His words? Repeating them over and over again?"

Chanting, the boy remembered.

"His words," she continued, "they made it writhe." She looked away from the dying half of the bundle to the leftovers the boy forgot about. The writhing thing he stabbed. The boy remembered it then. He was remembering a lot now, but it all came in pieces, too many things at once, but they had happened as fast as they came to him.

"It...*he* was changing." she said and looked at the boy, "But you stopped it from changing. You cured it."

She said nothing else, but he understood the things her expression told him. There was a question of how he did it. Then a sure guess as to how he did it. A quick denial and then a consideration of acceptance. A sense of foolishness of entertaining that acceptance, and then a consideration of asking him if he would act one more time. Then there was foolishness again toward that consideration.

She ended with stopping at a crossroad, unable to decide.

Was he to decide?

Then it would be easier. He knew what he wouldn't do, but she needed to hear it, didn't she?

"How did I do it?" he said. "I didn't cure him."

"But you did." she said.

"I killed him." he corrected.

A pause for shock, but a brave attempt to press the issue as though there was a positive way to approach it.

"Was it so simple?" she asked.

"Killing him? No." he said.

"Not killing him." she said. "Curing him."

"Is he cured?" he asked.

She looked over at the thing that once writhed, "He is. He's a man lying there." She looked at the boy. "They are men. They started as men." She looked over at the black half of the bundle, "Then he convinced them they weren't."

The boy looked at the dying figure. "So, it *is* nothing but a trick?"

"No," she said and looked at the boy, "It's real. It's a curse. The words he speaks, they rearrange things."

"Rearrange?" he asked.

She smirked, "All men have a beast within them. You've witnessed this first hand."

"The ones we killed." he said and then tensed, turning his head up to gaze toward the center of the cave, "Are there any of them...?"

She pressed her hand to his cheek and turned his face back to hers. "The one you killed."

He considered her statement and then was realigned with her previous statement. It was then he felt the dampness between her hand and his cheek. He knew what it was and that it might have been his...or it might have been theirs.

"There are none but us left." she said. "You and I."

"The copies?" he asked.

"Their job is done."

"So they...?"

"No." she shook her head. "Just you and I. Only us."

"But...but they..."

"Were only distractions." she said. "They could do nothing more."

"So they didn't..."

"No." she said. "Just you and me."

The entire cave painted in blood and bodies, the two of them alone, accompanied by nothing more than shadows.

But how? She was no surprise, but himself? He was no warrior, and yet...and yet...

"But you are able to call off the beast." she said. "His words, they make the beast and the outward man trade places, and that is when the manifestations appear. Though, the man now within can't always be suppressed, so they walk upon the border of both, having humanity but wanting the beast. To have the beast, they learn tricks. The tricks are for them, but mostly for those who see them. The only way to be a beast is to be feared. When people believe in the tricks, they fear, satisfying these poor men."

"Well, then," the boy said, "you just have to convince yourself otherwise, right?"

The girl said nothing, faced with a simple answer, unable to believe it to be so easy, and yet hoping a simple solution could be possible. She couldn't accept it, though, and shook her head. "It's not just in the words but in the knife as well."

When she saw his confusion, she crawled away from him to pick up the dagger that once tried to take his life. She sat with her legs curled and showed him the blade. The blade was double-edged, and the center of it adorned green flakes that looked like glass.

"In order to live another life, your first life must die." she said. "With this knife, the curse enters the blood, the saliva, a person's being. Their mind is of the beast. The words help the process along."

The boy remembered he was about to be stabbed by it before she tackled the figure. "Who is he?" he asked.

She looked over her shoulder at the dying bundle, "A shaman of dark arts."

The boy scrambled to his feet, "If it's poison then there's an antidote."

He was standing over the dark shaman before she could stop him. He snatched the front of the shaman's robes and yanked him up from the cave floor. The shaman hung limp in his grip.

"You understand me. You've been beaten. Tell me how to turn it around."

The shaman lifted his head enough to roll his eyes down at the boy.

"How?" the boy hissed. "How do we stop it? How do we reverse it?"

The shaman's parted lips turned into a gapped smile, exposing his toothless gums. He began to gurgle a chuckle.

"Tell me!" the boy snapped.

The shaman's lips tried to close to form a certain syllable. He tried to keep his smile, though, while he staggered the word, "B....b-b...b-beeaaa...sssst."

His eyes widened as if to emphasize the boy as his target, "Beeeaassssssst."

The beast she was talking about. The boy gritted his teeth and clenched his other fist, waking the handkerchief claw into its shape on his finger. He readied it, "Do you want to see it that badly?"

The shaman uttered his gaped mouthed chuckle again.

She clasped the boy's weaponized forearm, drawing his attention. Her ghostly eyes were settled on his. "Remember what I said about his words? Are you going to let him lure you in as well?"

"But...but what about the...?"

"Why would he have an antidote when he believes in this so much?" she asked.

His shoulders sagged. "Then what do we do?" he hissed.

She stared at him a moment until she gathered up the courage to speak, "The way the process goes. Only one way. You've followed through with it."

"What do you mean?" he asked.

"If one has to give up one life to lead another, then..."

He released the shaman who dropped with a cough upon the cave floor. "You're asking for death."

She was, she realized. "Is there another way?"

"You said before that we'd both walk out of here together." he snapped.

"You remember what I said to you before all this?" she asked. "As soon as you were finished, I told you to leave here."

"And you'd meet me." he added.

"How long would you have to wait, I wonder?" she asked.

"I'm not waiting." he said. "We're going out together."

"With me being the way I am?" she asked.

He ran his hand through his hair with a scoff and then threw his arm down by his side, "What's wrong with the way you are?" he asked.

They stared at each other then, feeling the quiet of the cave.

He could tell he caught her off guard. He also saw that she was trying to work up some response.

"What have you got to say?" he demanded.

"You expect me to stay like this forever?" she asked.

"You act like it's something you can't handle." he said. "If I can suppress the beast, then so can you, regardless of some poison." He pointed at her with his free hand, "And didn't you mention before in my town, to me and to all those people listening that people have called you things before? Things like monster and demon and such? What's the difference now? So you are an animal? So what? It's just another one of your tricks, right? You're a magician. You've challenged another. You've learned a trick. You've decided to change from your experience, adorning the change as a trophy. You already have an exotic appearance about you. So, you're the same, right?"

Silence.

"Right?" he snapped.

There was a smile on her face he didn't notice until now. It soothed his mounting rage. His face relaxed, and he studied her smile.

"Exotic." she said.

"What?" he asked.

"You said...I looked exotic?"

The boy blushed and glanced away, scratching at his cheek, "Oh, well, yeah, I mean, you do have a unique..." He stopped when he noticed her approaching. She pressed herself against him and embraced him. Again, he hadn't expected this from her and was slow to react. Though, he eventually folded his arms around her.

She snickered when he did. "You're a crafty young man."

"Why do you say that?" he asked.

"Your idea. It's sound." she said. "And I'm reminded of what you said earlier."

"When?"

"Before we decided to hunt down our adversary." she said. "There, out in the field, you told those men their tricks were indeed tricks. You helped me remember who I am. What I am. Just like you have now. I'm a wicked magician, aren't I?"

He chuckled. "I don't know about wicked, but..."

"Oh, come on." she said, moving back a bit to look him in the face, "I'm covered in the blood of my victims."

"So am I." he said.

She studied his face anew, "You feel you've changed?"

"Not really." he said, "But like you said, I have potential."

She smiled, "You are somewhat of a magician yourself, you know?"

"Am I?" he asked.

"A magician is a crafty one." she said. "And you're definitely crafty."

"So," he said, "does that mean you'll come back with me?"

She tilted her head to the side, curious, "You really want me to come back? You think I can?"

"Well, you told those people you'd bring back proof, right?" the boy said. "Show them your fangs. Tell them it's nothing more than a trick. They'll believe you because you're there in their presence, and you're not trying to eat them."

She laughed at that, and he spotted her glinting fangs, but they didn't bother him. Not anymore.

"And then what?" she asked, arching her eyebrows.

"Then you entertain us." he said.

"Is that all?" she asked.

"Isn't that what you came to do?" he asked.

"True," she said, "but things don't always happen like you think, do they?"

He shrugged, "So you got a little sidetracked."

"And then reigned back in by my young hero." she said.

He blushed and remembered they were still in each other's arms.

"How long should I stay, I wonder?" she asked.

He shrugged again, "As long as you want."

"And when that time is up?" she asked.

"Then you're off on another adventure."

"And you?" she asked, her voice a little quieter, her expression more relaxed.

"Me? I'll be a magician by that time." he said.

"Will you?" she asked, her eyebrows shooting up again.

"And you'll have to challenge me."

She smiled from ear to ear, "You've got this all planned out, don't you, crafty one?"

"Maybe I do." he said.

"Well," she laughed, "looks like you might've pulled one over on me."

He smiled, "Said the magician who bewitched me from the beginning."

www.ingramcontent.com/pod-product-compliance
Lightning Source LLC
Chambersburg PA
CBHW021901170526
45157CB00005B/1908